RIGVEDA – IN A NUTSHELL

DR. JAGADEESH PILLAI

Dedicated to Vedic Literature Lovers

Contents

Contents

Prayer

Ganga tharanga ramaneeya jata kalapam,
Gowri niranthara vibhooshitha vama bhagam,
Narayana priya mananga madapaharam,
Varanasi pura pathim Bhajha Viswanatham ||

About The Author

Dr. Jagadeesh Pillai four times Guinness World Record holder, a voracious reader, writer, and true research scholar was born in Varanasi, the abode of Lord Shiva. He is Ph.D. in Vedic Science. He is a multi-faceted polymath with innate qualities, creative ideas and many remarkable achievements. Although his roots extend back to "Gods own Country"(Kerala), the residents of Varanasi feel proud of him and adore him as a child of Varanasi who caters to every individual in need without any expectations. A deep study into his profile reflects that he has added so many feathers to his cap which makes him quite unique. He is a four times Guinness Book of World Records Holder in the following subjects :

1. "Script to Screen" which he achieved by producing and directing a state of art animation film within the shortest time possible by breaking the earlier set record by Canadians. There are many national and international Awards and Recognitions to his credit.

2. Longest Line of Post Cards which he has done on the occasion of 163 years of Indian Postal Day by 16300 post cards. The event was also connected with a questionnaire about Indian Flag.

3. Largest Poster Awareness Campaign – This was achieved by designing an awareness campaign on the subject "Beti Bachao – Beti Padhao".

4. Largest Envelop – Towards tribute to Prime Minister's

initiative 'Make in India' – he has created about 4000 sq meter envelop using waste papers.

5. Attempted by lighting 70000 candles on a 210 kg cake to celebrate the 70th Indian Independence day recorded in World Records India.

6. Attempted a documentary on Dhamek Stupa of Sarnath dubbing in 17 languages, result is waiting from Guinness World Records.

He is versatile in Gita teaching. The young generation is fond of his Gita teaching and he has changed the life of many young through his continued motivational boost up and teachings.

He has composed and sung Gayatri Mantra in 1008 different tunes.

He has composed and sung Hanuman Chalisa in 108 different tunes.

He has composed and sung hundreds of Sanskrit Bhajans, Patriotic songs, etc.

He has written and directed so many short films and documentaries for awareness campaigns.

He has done voluntary services to UP Police and Kerala Police to spread awareness campaigns on the various issue through videos and photography.

He is on the path of authoring thousands of books on Indian culture, Indian Temples, and the life of extraordinary people.

It is hard to believe that he has produced and directed more than 100 Documentaries on a particular city (Varanasi) which is done by a single person.

He has helped and guided more than 25 boys and girls to achieve world records through various creative and innovative methods.

A multifaceted person who can apply the best of his intellect using the God-given blessings which have been showered upon every human being granting them an immense capacity to learn, experience, and experiment with many things and do wonders in this world of discrimination and disparities.

He is a teacher and a student at the same time who always learns every day and teaches every day. As a master, his weakness was that he never sticks to a particular subject. Perhaps this weakness gives him the strength to master any area which he came across.

Each of his days dawned with learning a new topic and he spend most of his time experimenting and researching it.

He is also a selfless social activist and a motivational speaker.

His life was full of struggle, ups and downs, and failures.

But he never gave up and faced all his trials and tribulations full of confidence. Today he is a successful young man with a lot of enthusiasm and rich life experience.

He has sung full Ram Charita Manas 51 hours audio by his own composition. He has also sung the whole Bhagavad-Gita in his own composition with a rhythmic background.

He has also sung "Lokah Samastha Sukhino Bhavantu" in 50 different languages.

Currently working on a detailed and scientific study on Veda, Upanishad, Puranas, Bhagavad Gita, etc.

He has composed and sung Hanuman Chalisa in 108 different compositions and Gayatri Mantra in 1008 different compositions.

Awards

Four Times Guinness World Records

Winner of Mahatma Gandhi Vishwa Shanti Puraskar

Mahatma Gandhi Global Peace Ambassador

Kashi Ratna Award

Dr. APJ Abdul Kalam Motivational Person of the Year 2017

Mother Teresa Award

Indira Gandhi Priyadarshini Award

Bharat Vikas Ratna Award

Udyog Ratna Award

Vigyan Prasar Award

Poorvanchal Ratn Samman

Preface

The Rigveda is the first of the Vedic texts, each of which holds its own significance. The Rigveda is an ancient collection of hymns and other religious texts that are believed to have been composed between 1500 and 1200 BCE. It is the oldest surviving Indian text and is considered to be the foundation of Hinduism. The Rigveda is composed of 10 books, each containing hymns and other religious texts. These hymns are believed to have been composed by various sages and are dedicated to various gods and goddesses. The Rigveda is an important source of knowledge about the Vedic period and provides insight into the beliefs and practices of the ancient Indians. It is also an important source of information about the gods and goddesses of the Vedic period. The Rigveda is an invaluable source of knowledge and is essential for understanding the history and culture of ancient India.

I have attempted to provide a brief overview of the importance of the Rigveda here.

CHAPTER ONE

RIGVEDA - INTRODUCTION

The Rigveda is one of the oldest surviving collections of sacred texts in world history, a part of the larger body of Vedic literature. It is believed to have been composed between 1500 to 1000 BCE in the northwestern region of India. This sacred collection comprises 1,028 hymns dedicated to a pantheon of deities, offering insight into the spiritual beliefs, rituals, and customs of the Vedic people of the time.

The Rigveda is divided into ten books, each of which is further split into several hymns. Many of the hymns are addressed to specific gods and goddesses, primarily Indra and Agni, the gods of storm and fire, respectively. The offerings made to these gods often take the form of a yajña, or a sacrifice made on behalf of the divine. Each offering is carefully prepared to give thanks and appease the gods, with prayers and mantras performed as part of the ritual.

The hymns also provide an insight into the daily lives of the Vedic people, as they talk of various aspects of their daily lives, such as battles and migration, religious rituals, and the importance of livestock. The hymns are filled with poetic words and imagery, which help the reader to understand the richness of the Vedic culture.

The tone of the hymns often varies, either praising the gods with joyous prayers and detailed descriptions of the offerings to be made, or with humbler supplications to them. The Rigveda also contains strains of philosophy and discussions on the importance of dharma, or a moral and ethical code.

The structure of the Rigveda is also quite unique, with the verses composed in a specific meter, or chant, to be sung during the ritual offerings. This form of rhythmic chanting is said to have an immensely calming effect, and has been known to be used in later Hindu religious literature as well.

It is believed that the Rigveda was the first and most important of the four Vedas, influencing the Hindu traditions and beliefs to this day. Its ancient language and intricate structure shows the dedication and love with which the Vedic priests penned the hymns, and remains a great source of wisdom and knowledge.

CHAPTER TWO

VERSES OF RIGVEDA

The Rigveda is the oldest and most important of the four Vedas, the oldest of the Hindu religious texts. Since its compilation in India around 1500 BCE, the Rigveda has become the most widely studied of all the ancient Indian texts. It is one of the most important sources of Hindu culture and tradition, and has been the source of religious, spiritual, and literary inspiration for countless generations of Hindus.

Unlike the other Vedas, the Rigveda does not provide an analysis of the Hindu religious system as a whole. Instead, the Rigveda focuses on the individual, personal aspects of Hinduism, such as ritualistic devotion, the formation of various ritualistic procedures, and the philosophy behind suggested actions. In this regard, the Rigveda stands out from the other Vedas by being more focused on the individual than on the divine

The Rigveda is also unique in its composition. Unlike the other Vedas, which have been compiled as collections of hymns and sung by trained singers, the Rigveda is composed entirely in prose. This prose form, known as the kanda-stuti, allows the Rigveda to better explain its intricate doctrines, rituals, and metaphysical concepts. In addition, since the Rigveda is composed in prose, the texts are often disjointed and lack the narrative structure of the other three Vedas

The Rigveda's emphasis on the individual is also seen in its many hymns. While the other Vedas are filled with hymns praising various deities and states of being, the Rigveda often focuses on personal achievement and worldly success. This emphasis on individual reward is also seen in its stories, which are often centered on human experiences rather than divine

In addition, the Rigveda is heavily focused on philosophy. Metaphysical concepts can be seen throughout the text, and the Rigveda's emphasis on introspection and contemplation allows its readers to question and explore its teachings. The other Vedas, by comparison, are less focused on the philosophical, concentrating more on a moral code of conduct

Finally, the Rigveda is unique in its form. While the other Vedas are composed of verse and meter, the Rigveda is composed in prose. This form allows for a more in-depth exploration of its teachings, as it allows for greater description and more complex arguments. As a result, the Rigveda is able to provide a more comprehensive understanding of the Hindu worldview

In summary, the Rigveda is unique in its approach to Hinduism and differs from the other Vedas in its focus on the individual, its lack of narrative structure, its emphasis on philosophical concepts, and its composition. This allows the Rigveda to provide a more detailed exploration of the Hindu worldview and its consequences.

CHAPTER THREE

RISHIES OF RIGVEDA

The Rigveda is one of the oldest pieces of literature in the world, dating back to as early as the 2nd millennium BCE. This ancient collection of over 1028 hymns, composed in ancient Sanskrit and attributed to various rishis, is one of the foundational scriptures of Hinduism. The Rigvedic rishis, referred to as maharishis or great sages, have been revered among generations of Indians for their divine knowledge.

The Vedic rishis were believed to possess divine inspiration and a deep understanding of the cosmic energies such as the "mantras" or spiritual powers (Rigveda X.82.9). The mantras, originating from the Rigveda, are mantras which are believed to unlock cosmic energy and direct it to help improve human life, enable spiritual knowledge, and influence the weather patterns and other events in the environment

The rishis of the Rigveda also believed in the use of meditation to channelize their inner wisdom and spiritual energy. They used meditation to help them reach a deep sense of understanding and ultimately bring their ideas to fruition. It is said that the mental images used by them during meditation were derived from the Rigveda's essential themes of deep cosmic understanding, the nature of Brahman, and its relationship to the cosmos. One of the most famous rishis of the Rigveda was Agastya, who was said to have divided the original Sanskrit texts of the Rigveda into four parts

The Rigvedic rishis are also renowned for their contributions to the Vedic sciences such as astronomy and mathematics. The earliest recorded "solar calendar" is said to have been developed by the Rigvedic rishis, who studied the sky with great detail and studied the motions of the stars, formulating an understanding of the various cycles the universe was engaged in. This was believed to be a key element for the ancient Indians in engaging with planetary movements and in devising a way to time events and religious festivals

In conclusion, the rishis of the Rigveda created one of the oldest and most influential Vedic literatures in the world. Their contributions to the Vedic sciences and understanding of human life was priceless, as was the determination and dedication with which they studied the cosmos and its energies. They were the sages and visionaries who truly carried the knowledge of the sacred Rigveda to the ancient Indians and continue to be among the most revered spiritual teachers of our time.

CHAPTER FOUR

RIGVEDIC BRAHMANS AND MANTRA CHANTING

The Rigvedic Brahmins are an ancient class of people in ancient India who dedicated their lives and work to the Rigveda, one of the oldest and most central religious texts in the Hindu tradition. They were unique amongst the various other classes of religious specialists because of their exclusive dedication to the Rigveda and to the interaction with the Veda gods and goddesses.

The Rigvedic Brahmins were central to the spread of Vedic culture and teachings throughout India, though there is little information about their origins or practices. It is known however, that they were highly respected figures in Vedic society, often performing royal and priestly duties. They acted as advisors to kings and performed all the rituals associated with the religion and daily life. As religious practitioners, they were responsible for the preservation and interpretation of the Rigvedic mantras and hymns which are so prominent in Hinduism today

Rigvedic Brahmins were also known for their chanting of Rigvedic mantras. This chanting is centered around the understanding that all of creation is a manifestation of the divine, and that everything is saturated by this all-pervading truth. The chanting of the Rigvedic mantras is an attempt to connect and be in tune with this truth. The mantras mediate and are meant to be chanted in line with the cosmic rhythm and can be used both as an invocation of divine energies as well as for healing purposes

Additionally, there were many other practices undertaken by the Rigvedic Brahmins. They performed ritual sacrifices, served as priests to the gods and goddesses, and practiced meditation and yoga. The Rigvedic Brahmins were also the guardians of Vedic law, and they served as philosophers, teachers, and mediators of the human and divine realms

Overall, the Rigvedic Brahmins were a key part of the early Hindu tradition, as they not only kept the religious practices alive and maintained the traditions but also spread Vedic teachings throughout India. The Rigvedic mantras they chanted and passed down through the generations continue to be a part of the religion today, and help promote the understanding that all of creation is a divine expression.

CHAPTER FIVE

DEVATAS OF RIGVEDA

The Devatas of Rigvedic Mantra Verses are spiritual entities mentioned in the Vedic scriptures of ancient India. These Devatas are believed to possess supernatural powers and are responsible for creating, sustaining and protecting the universe, as well as controlling all the forces of nature. They are seen as the manifestation of cosmic powers, taking on a variety of forms such as gods, goddesses, demons, and other supernatural beings

One of the most important aspects of these Devatas is their connection to the Rigvedic mantras. These mantras are powerful formulas found within the Vedic texts that invoke the Devatas' assistance and bring them into existence. These mantras are believed to contain spiritual information that is essential for human enlightenment, and are said to manifest the Devatas and their power to the physical world. It is believed that those who are able to recite these mantras properly will experience the gifts and blessings of these Devatas

The Rigveda includes hundreds of such mantras, and each one invokes a specific Devata for assistance. Devatas such as Agni, Indra, Ushanas, and Vayu are invoked in mantras to bring health, abundance, protection, and prosperity. The mantras are believed to have the power to transform and bring about spiritual growth. These mantras are also used for healing and protection from demonic influences

The Devatas of Rigvedic Mantra Verses represent a variety of divine powers, and it is believed that they are capable of guiding the souls of humans along their life path. By reciting these mantras and invoking the presence of these Devatas, one can receive spiritual guidance and protection, leading to a more meaningful life. They can also act as the bridge between earthly existence and spiritual bliss

The increasing popularity of Vedic scriptures in the modern world has seen an increasing interest in the Devatas of Rigvedic Mantra Verses. Through the use of these mantras and the invocation of their powers, many people have experienced profound spiritual transformation and healing. These Devatas represent the cosmic force and bring balance to life. It is believed that through the correct pronunciation of these mantras, one can experience a direct connection to the higher powers and receive guidance in their life endeavors.

RIGVEDA MANTRA AND DAY TO DAY LIFE

The Rig Veda is a collection of hymns and verses that were composed by ancient Vedic seers and have been passed down orally for thousands of years in India. The Rig Veda is considered to be the oldest of the four Hindu religious texts known as the Vedas, and is still revered as the oldest sacred book.

Rik Veda mantras are an integral part of Hinduism and have been used by Hindus throughout the ages for spiritual, mental and physical health, and for worship. Rik Veda mantras are rich with the language of the Vedic rishis, and are chanted in certain specific rhythms and tones. They offer the mind and soul a vessel for spiritual experience and enlightenment.

The Rik Veda mantras are used for all kinds of worship, ranging from praying for peace and joy in the home, to healing, to mind and soul purification. Each mantra from the Rig Veda has a unique vibration and purpose, and each has its own special use in the spiritual journey. In addition to being used for worship, the Rik Veda mantras are also used for various healing treatments, such as sound and crystal therapy, Ayurveda, and meditation.

The word "mantra" itself has many meanings but primarily refers to the repetition of a word or phrase in order to attain a certain goal or to develop a certain state of mind. Rik Veda mantras have a vast range of uses, such as to help invoke certain deities and uphold values, to attract positive energies and get rid of negative energies, to achieve a state of mindfulness, and to simply create a peaceful and calm atmosphere. Their use in day-to-day life and worship can be seen in many traditional Hindu practices such as puja ceremonies and the offering of flowers and fruits to deities.

Often, these mantras are chanted while meditating or during meditation retreats, and they have an immense power to heal, purify, and raise the vibration of the atmosphere. To some, Rik Veda mantras are synonymous with the Vedic tradition itself, and the chanting of these mantras can help a person tap into the deep roots of the Vedic tradition of yoga, ethics and spiritual enlightenment.

One of the most important aspects of Rik Veda mantras is that they are used to connect to the Supreme Being, or Brahman. When chanted in the right manner and with the proper intention, these mantras can serve as a gateway to Brahman. This connection to Brahman is said to bring a feeling of peace and contentment, which in turn can bring spiritual growth, health, and prosperity.

In conclusion, the Rik Veda mantras are an integral part of Hinduism and serve as powerful tools for day-to-day living and worship. Used correctly, these mantras can bring peace and harmony and connect an individual to the Supreme Being.

CHAPTER SEVEN

MODERN APPROACH TO RIGVEDA

The Rigveda is one of the most ancient Hindu texts, predating Christianity by thousands of years. It is composed of over 1,000 hymns, ranging in topics from praise of the gods to the rituals of the gods. Its primary purpose is to offer spiritual guidance to those who follow it. In today's world, however, many individuals find it difficult to access and interpret the Rigveda due to its complexity.

Fortunately, there is a modern approach to studying the Rigveda which is far more accessible for individuals. This modern approach focuses on the idea of cultural relativism, which states that all cultures should be respected and seen as valid, regardless of their age or origin. This emphasis on respect for tradition has allowed for the Rigveda to be better understood and appreciated

Further, this modern approach has emphasized the importance of critical engagement with the Rigveda. Instead of simply viewing it as a set of ancient rules, the text is now often studied and discussed for its deeper philosophical meanings and its application to the modern world. Numerous academic papers have been written about the Rigveda and its ideas, allowing for greater appreciation of its many layers

In addition, this modern approach has encouraged the use of other, non-traditional sources in order to gain an understanding of the Rigveda. Although the traditional texts are still revered, modern-day scholars have embraced additional sources such as archaeological evidence, contemporary writing, and even songs in order to get a better sense of the text's original context. This inclusivity helps to paint a more vivid picture of the Rigveda and the world it was composed in.

Overall, this modern approach to the Rigveda has made the text much more accessible and interesting to those who study it. It has shifted the focus from blind obedience to critical engagement, allowing individuals to appreciate the text on a deeper level. By combining traditional sources with contemporary perspectives, more meaningful interpretations of the text can be gained. By paying homage to the ancients but still engaging with the Rigveda for its relevance in the modern world, its ancient messages can truly be seen and appreciated.

CHAPTER EIGHT

RIGVEDA SCHOOLS

Rigveda is one of the four sacred texts of ancient India, and is the oldest of these texts. It is believed to have been compiled in Sanskrit around 1500 BC, making it one of the oldest known works of literature. The Rigveda contains hymns and prayers written in praise of the various elements of nature, mainly the gods and goddesses. The Rigveda is also a source of great spiritual knowledge, and as such, it has been used as the basis for many spiritual schools across India.

Rigveda Schools are spiritual institutions dedicated to the teachings of the Rigveda. These schools are among the oldest institutions of higher learning in India, as they trace their roots back to the Vedic period itself.

Rigveda schools place great emphasis on the study and practice of Vedic philosophy and culture. Their curriculum focuses on the reading and interpretation of the hymns and prayers found in the Rigveda, as well as their application in balanced living. Rigveda Schools promote a calm, contemplative lifestyle, free from destructive worldly practises.

In order to become a part of a Rigveda School, students must meet various requirements set out by the school. These can include a basic knowledge of Sanskrit, a commitment to the values and lifestyle of the school, and a willingness to adhere to a strict schedule. Students are expected to maintain a high level of academic excellence, as the rigours of the school's curriculum demand it.

The learning environment in Rigveda Schools is quite unique. Everyday life in the schools is characterised by meditation, contemplation, and prayer. Students are expected to perform certain daily rituals and observe certain regulations while in the school. These include observing fasts and abstaining from certain foods and activities that may conflict with the values associated with the Rigveda.

Rigveda Schools have been a major influence in the spiritual and philosophical development of India, and are nowadays much sought after. The rigours and commitment expected of their students are great, but so are the rewards - spiritual knowledge, inner peace and a life of devotion.

CHAPTER NINE

RIGVEDA AND UPANISHAD

The Rigveda and Upanishads are two of the most important works of Hindu literature, with a shared yet distinct history. The Rigveda is an ancient collection of Vedic sacred hymns, composed in Vedic Sanskrit and written in the early part of the 1st Millennium BCE. It is considered to be one of the oldest religious texts in the world and is the source of many philosophical and religious ideas found in Hinduism and other Indian religions. The Upanishads, on the other hand, are a collection of Vedic texts, composed sometime in the mid 1st Millennium BCE, dealing with the metaphysical and cosmological aspects of life and the nature of existence. Both works constitute the Vedas, or knowledge, of Hinduism and are presently revered as the backbone of Hindu philosophy, albeit with different emphasis.

The Rigveda, which is composed of 10 books or mandalas, is considered to be the earliest of the Hindu scriptures, providing the basic structure for further religious thought and spiritual traditions of India. The bulk of these hymns are about the gods, particularly Indra and Agni, and prayers addressed to them, together with suggestions for their propitiation. These hymns also include descriptions of natural phenomena, from the movement of the sun to the growth of plants and animals, as well as genetic concepts of creation which speak to a gradual development rather than a singular moment of creation. The Rigveda also contains themes of social and moral rectitude, as well as suggesting the newly-forming Indian society's ideas of fairness and justice.

The Upanishads, while closely connected to the Vedic literature and mythology, move in a different direction. These works are concerned with the nature of existence and how to experience freedom through understanding, providing insight into the innermost self and emphasizing the importance of knowledge and contemplation. Interestingly, there seems to be an emergence of a new concept of God, who is greater than the Vedic pantheon follows, with a greater focus on the individual, rather than the rituals and sacrifices prescribed by the Vedas. The Upanishads also introduce the concepts of karma, rebirth, and liberation, which are now staples of the Hindu religion.

In sum, the Rigveda and the Upanishads, while closely related, differ significantly in several respects. The Rigveda affirms the dominant Vedic mythology and celebrates the gods, while the Upanishads are concerned with liberation and understanding of the self, thus opening the door for more complex religious thought over time. Despite their differences, however, the Rigveda and Upanishads are commonly seen as two parts of one whole and are revered as an essential part of the Hindu tradition.

DR. JAGADEESH PILLAI

CHAPTER TEN

RIGVEDA AND BHAGAVADGITA

The Rigveda and the Bhagavad Gita are among two of the most important and significant ancient scriptures of Hinduism. As a part of their moral, spiritual and religious significance and resonance, they have great influence in terms of framing the foundations of philosophy and religion of the religion. Despite their differences in themes, the two scriptures have a common origin and share the same fundamental teachings and principles.

The Rigveda is one of the oldest Vedic scriptures in the Hindu religion, and is especially revered for being the sacred source of truth for Hindus. It is of great historical and spiritual significance, as it offers an insight into the earliest beliefs and rituals of Hindus. The Rigveda is a collection of hymns that are used as a means of expressing gratitude and praise to the divine forces. The 10th mandala of the Rigveda is known as the "Adhyatma Mandala" and it is this part of the scripture that offers the most insight into the Hindu religion. It houses key teachings on topics such as the importance of knowledge, the divine nature of the soul, and the importance of self-realization.

On the other hand, the Bhagavad Gita is a part of the Hindu epic, the Mahabharata. It is considered to be the most important scripture of Hinduism after the Vedas. It is especially significant due to its teachings of transcendental knowledge and use of spiritual concepts such as karma and dharma. The Bhagavad Gita is not so much a philosophical treatise as it is a text about spirituality, morality, and the pursuit of moksha (liberation). It serves as a gateway between the physical and spiritual worlds, offering many valuable lessons about the human condition and the nature of ultimate reality.

Despite the obvious differences between them, the Rigveda and the Bhagavad Gita still share a common origin and can be said to be connected to each other in some way. The Rigveda, being one of the earliest Vedic scriptures, can be seen as a source of philosophy and religion that is shared by both the Rigveda and the Bhagavad Gita. Both scriptures come from the same oral tradition, and have influenced each other's teachings in some way or another. The Rigveda, through its emphasis on knowledge and the importance of understanding the divine, offers important insights and concepts that can help in understanding the teachings of the Bhagavad Gita. On the other hand, the Bhagavad Gita also has lessons and ideas that are relevant to the Rigveda, such as the importance of living a life in accordance with the law of karma and the need to strive for liberation.

Ultimately however, it is the concept of Brahman (the Supreme Being) that binds both the Rigveda and the Bhagavad Gita together.

CHAPTER ELEVEN

RIGVEDA AND PURANAS

The Rigveda and the Puranas have been integral aspects of Indian culture for thousands of years. This ancient literature can be considered a source of divine knowledge, offering us a moral and spiritual compass for guidance and enlightenment in our lives. To understand their relationship we must first understand what each is and how they are related.

The Rigveda is an ancient religious text consisting of 1,028 hymns devoted to various deities. It is the oldest Indian scripture and among the most sacred Hindu texts. The subject matter of each hymn varies from spiritual wisdom to sacrifice rituals, from astrological readings to prayers for divine aid.

Puranas, on the other hand, are ancient scriptures, composed in Sanskrit and containing stories about various Hindu gods and goddesses. Puranas are much less serious in tone, often containing moral lessons, advice and wisdom rather than religious services. They range in length from 18,000 verses to over 270,000 verses.

The Rigveda and the Puranas are closely related, as they both contain stories and wisdom derived from the Vedic period. While the Rigveda focuses on the spiritual aspects of Hinduism, the Puranas offer us moral lessons and advice, making them both integral components of the entire Vedic corpus.

One of the most significant ways in which they are connected is through the use of names and deities. Many Rigvedic hymns are devoted to particular Vedic gods and goddesses, whose stories and deeds feature in the Puranas too. So, for example, the Rigveda hymns of Indra praise the great god for his heroic deeds and military prowess, while the Puranas recount these deeds in greater detail and provide larger stories about Indra's life and adventures.

Additionally, the development of Hinduism has been highly influenced by what was written in the Rigveda and the Puranas. The Vedic gods and goddesses as well as stories and rituals described in the primeval works of the Rigveda and the Puranas shaped the customs, beliefs and spiritual tenets of the Hindus, consequently making both of these unique scriptures pillars of faith and spiritual guidance.

The Rigveda and the Puranas are thus deeply connected and complementary in nature. They both served as a source of inspiration and teachings for the Hindu faith and way of life for thousands of years, and their influence and importance continue to this day.

CHAPTER TWELVE

RIGVEDA AND FIVE ELEMENTS

Rigveda is an ancient collection of Sanskrit texts that form a part of the Vedic religion and culture of the Indian subcontinent. It is composed of 10 mandalas or books, containing a total of 10,552 mantras or hymns - some of which are the oldest literature in the world. The Rigveda is based on the belief that all creation is composed of five elements: air (vayu), water (jala), fire (agni), earth (bhumi), and space (akasha).

The emphasis on the five elements in the Rigveda is clear, not only in terms of its composition, but also in terms of many features of its ritual or religious practices. For instance, in the ancient Hindu ritual of yajna, the priests used fire and the five elements to make offerings to the gods. In general, the rituals were much more elaborate than what we see today.

In terms of its mantras, many Rigvedic verses explicitly mention the five elements. The fifth mandala of the Rigveda, for instance, contains a hymn praising the five elements, with a focus on the aspect of fire. Similarly, a mantra from the seventh mandala speaks of the importance of all five elements in the ritual of yajna. Finally, another hymn from the fourth mandala articulates the cosmic role of the five elements in Vedic cosmology.

In the Rigvedic culture, mantras were used to invoke the gods and invoke special requests or blessings. A mantra could also be used to honor the five elements, as their presence is essential to the completion of any ritual. It was believed that these mantras could bring about a harmonious balance in the universe.

The connection between Rigveda and the five elements is thus one of the key foundations of Hinduism. The Vedic worldview held that the five elements are at the core of the universe and its workings, and that they are essential to living a good life. The mantras of the Rigveda, by honoring and invoking these elements, help bring us into communion with them and with the divine realms. They serve as reminders of the power of cosmos and of the great interconnectedness of all creation.

CHAPTER THIRTEEN

RIGVED AND UNIVERSE

Rigveda, the oldest of the Vedic scriptures, is one of the foundational texts of Hinduism. Written in Sanskrit, it is composed of more than 1000 hymns, which are said to depict the connection between the universe and the divine. Rigveda mantra plays a central role in Hindu ritual and spiritual practices, serving as a form of communication and connection between the human and divine realms.

The Rigveda mantras are said to possess the power to unlock a deeper understanding of the universe, as well as providing insight and guidance for living a meaningful life. The hymns are composed in a poetic form, depicting various aspects of the divine, ranging from the creation of the universe to the nature of good and evil, as well as its ultimate redemption from suffering. Each hymn or mantra is believed to possess its own power and to be able to be used in various ritualistic or spiritual practices.

Rigveda ritualistic practices, such as homas and yajnas, are typically performed with the help of mantras. These ceremonies are intended to bring a person closer to the divine, enabling them to access a deeper understanding of the true nature of the universe. For example, some of the Rigveda's mantras can be used to meditate on the oneness of the universe and to connect oneself with the divine. Other mantras help to clear away negative thoughts and can be used to achieve a mental state of calm and concentration.

Rigveda mantras also serve as an important part of Hindu religious festivals, such as the popular Navaratri festival. As part of the traditional worship, mantras are chanted in Sanskrit to honor various Hindu deities, along with various spiritual and mystical practices. During the rituals, the mantras are believed to help connect humans to the universal energy, ultimately leading to self-realization.

The Rigveda thus serves to provide a connection between humans and the universe. Its mantras and hymns serve as a powerful tool to understand and connect with the oneness of the universe. Through these prayers and hymns, it is believed that the power of the divine can be accessed, and that those who recite these mantras can discover the spiritual truths of life. Ultimately, the power of the Rigveda and its mantras serves to bring humans closer to the divine and to provide a deeper understanding of the universe.

CHAPTER FOURTEEN

RIGVEDA – INTERNATIONAL AUTHORS

The Rigveda is one of the oldest extant texts in the world, dating back to 1700-1100 BCE. It is a Sanskrit collection of hymns and verses thought to be composed by priest-sages, focused on spiritual and cosmic themes. It is one of the four primary texts of the Hindu religion, and its influence can be traced across many centuries and cultures.

The Rigveda has been studied and written about by many scholars across the globe, both traditional and modern. In the Indian subcontinent, some of the most noted ancient commentators of the Rigveda include the sage Yaska, the commentator Sayana, and the great Sanskrit grammarian Patanjali. Traditional works from the medieval period such as the Rigvedacchanda of Haradatta and Bhaskara's commentary also elucidate various aspects of the text.

Outside of India, the Rigveda has captivated and inspired many Western scholars. The first translation of the Rigveda in a European language was by Friedrich von Schlegel, a German scholar of the 19th century. This was followed by translations by other English scholars such as Max Mueller, Ralph T.H. Griffith, H.H. Wilson and A.A. Macdonell. Further works such as Gerald Larson's Rigveda, Works and Wendy Doniger's The Rigveda: An Anthology are also highly regarded in academia.

In the 20th century, many of the Rigveda's Sanskrit commentaries were translated into English. In 1914, Jules Barthélemy-Saint-Hilaire published a French translation of Sayana's commentary. And in the 1930s, G.A. Taine released an English version of the same. Other commentators whose works have been translated and annotated into English include the German scholar Hermann Oldenberg, whose prose translations and annotated texts of the Rigveda and the Atharvaveda have been highly influential.

Modern international scholars have also studied and written about various aspects of the Rigveda. In recent times, the renowned scholars Wendy Doniger and Michael Witzel have focused on the text and its literature. In her book, Jonathan Smith's Otherworld: Rigvedic Texts and Meanings, Doniger studies the imagery and ritual of the Rigveda, while Witzel explored the Vedic language and sacred texts in his paper "Vedic Hinduism: A Historical Perspective."

In general, the Rigveda continues to enthrall and inspire researchers and scholars around the world. From traditional commentators in India, to 19th-century European scholars, to contemporary writers, an eclectic range of international authors have studied, discussed, and written about the Rigveda and its literature.

CHAPTER FIFTEEN

MAX MUELLER AND RIGVEDA

Max Mueller was a German-born linguist and philologist who, during the 19th century, became renowned for his extensive work on the ancient Indian scripture known as the Rigveda. His research was instrumental in helping to shape the modern day understanding of Vedic Sanskrit, which is the oldest known dialect of the Sanskrit language.

Mueller was born in Dessau in 1823 and, following the death of his father, moved to England with his mother when he was eleven years old. He attended Oxford where he ultimately obtained a doctorate in Comparative Philology and Oriental Literature. It was around this time that he became intrigued by the Rigveda, and saw it as a way to understand the cultural and spiritual heritage of India. He initially published his research in 1860, which was the volume one of his translation of the Rigveda – or "Sacred Hymns of the Brahmans and Aryan Race" as it was titled.

Mueller set about carefully studying the Rigveda and learned Sanskrit and Vedic so that he could accurately study its contents. He also learned several other languages including Persian, Greek and Latin. He then devoted several years to working on his translation of the Rigveda, a sprawling and complex body of literature composed between 1700-1100 BC, comprising of more than 1000 Vedic Sanskrit hymns. In this unique project Mueller went beyond the usual philological approach which focuses exclusively on language and studied each hymn singly in order to gain an understanding of the religious, cultural and social contexts that provided the foundation for the hymn. This was an incredibly ambitious project because such an endeavour had never been attempted before.

Mueller's magnum opus, spanning seven volumes and nearly 3000 pages, was published between 1862–1882. His work was instrumental in developing an understanding of the Rigveda and of the structural aspects of its language. He was beloved not only in Germany but among Indian scholars as well, who recognized his efforts to carry out a very difficult endeavour.

Max Mueller's work on the Rigveda made an incredible contribution to our modern understanding of this ancient scripture, and his legacy still lives on today. He is considered one of the most important Indologists of the 19th century, and has left us a valuable legacy that continues to be studied and appreciated.

CHAPTER SIXTEEN

Ralph T.H. Griffith and Rigveda

Ralph T.H. Griffith was an Anglo-Irish Indologist and Sanskrit scholar during the 19th century. He is best known for his work on the Rigveda, the oldest of the four Vedas, one of the most ancient scriptures in Hinduism. Born in 1826, Griffith attained degrees in both English Literature and Biblical Studies at Trinity College, Oxford. His academic career was initially in the field of Christian studies and his first works were Bible translations in various Indian languages such as Bengali and Marathi.

It was only in 1854, upon arriving in India and becoming a Civil Servant with the Court of Benaras, that he took a great interest in Indology and particularly, in Hinduism. As such, Griffith decided to dedicate his career to the study of the Rigveda, the primary source of scripture for many Hindus. He was the first to unabridgedly translate the Rigveda into a western language, and this major undertaking would come to define his life's work.

Griffith worked for about twenty five years to perfect this ambitious project, for which he was allotted a generous stipend by the East India Company. In order to accurately study the mysterious Vedic language – which has been compared to a mixture of Old German and Old Slavonic – he enrolled to study Sanskrit at the Benaras Hindu University, studying under Ganganath Jha, an eminent Sanskrit scholar.

In 1861, the first volume of Griffith's translation of the Rigveda was published, containing 75 hymns and 1,017 verses, as well as three complete recensions of the old Sanskrit text with English commentaries and appendices. This was followed by the publication of the remaining seven volumes over the course of the following eleven years. These significant works explored the origin and contemporary knowledge of the Vedic practices and rituals, as well as their interpretation. As part of his research process, Griffith also tried to historicize the Rigveda. He used comparative philology and proposed that the Rigveda had been composed in Vedic Sanskrit and then polished in Classical Sanskrit. This highly-praised research and meticulous translation laid the foundation for the modern understanding of the Rigveda.

Griffith's translation attracted much renown, however it was not completely free from criticism. Unfortunately, some of the conclusions he had made were wrong, and there were inaccuracies in the phonological interpretation of the text. Furthermore, there were those who felt his translation was too presumptuous. Nevertheless, his work still stands as one of the most important contributions to Indology and modern religion, and his efforts to present the Rigveda with clarity and accuracy have been highly valued by many scholars and devotees. Ralph T.H. Griffith's work on the Rigveda changed the way we look at ancient Hindu scripture.

CHAPTER SEVENTEEN

AUTHOR H.H. WILSON AND RIGVEDA

H.H. Wilson (1786 - 1860) was an English orientalist, who was known for his pioneering work in the study of rigveda. He was the first person to make a serious English translation of the Rigveda, which has been acknowledged to be one of the most important books of the world's religion. Not just a scholar of the Indian scriptures, Wilson was also well-versed in Pali and Buddhist texts.

Wilson first made contact with the original text of the Rigveda in 1832, and for the next ten years he dedicated himself to studying and translating it. His translation was deeply researched and provided a comprehensive understanding of the text. Wilson considered the Rigveda to be the earliest work of its kind and the starting point for the history of ancient Indian literature. He treated the text reverentially, translating it word for word, rather than trying to reinterpret its content.

Wilson's translation was considered to be among the most accurate ever made of the text. He was also the first to treat the Rigveda as a true source of ancient religion, rather than just a book of rituals and incantations. He provided a significant commentary on the text, providing insight into the nature and functioning of the Vedic religion. Wilson drew attention to the different layers of meaning in the text, pointing out the various hymns, sacrificial instructions, and proverbs. He also combined his knowledge of the Sanskrit language with cultural and anthropological insights, to provide a comprehensive and informative approach to the Rigveda.

The critical work of Wilson on the Rigveda had a lasting impact on the field of Indology. His work gave western scholars and intellectuals a better understanding of the religious and philosophical scope of India. Further, his translation was seen as a major milestone in understanding India's ancient wisdom and contributed to the knowledge of Indian sciences and philosophies. Most importantly, Wilson's contribution opened the gateway to subsequent translations and interpretations of the Rigveda and provided the basis for further research into the ancient Indian texts.

In short, the pioneering work of H.H. Wilson on the Rigveda proved to be a significant turning point in the study of Indo-Muslim studies. His detailed and accurate translation of the sacred text has provided a comprehensive understanding of the Vedic religion and culture. Wilson's work continues to be an important source of knowledge and study in this field and his efforts remain highly respected among scholars of Indian religion and culture.

AUTHOR A.A. MACDONELL AND RIGVEDA

Author A.A. Macdonell is best known for his work on the Rigveda, an ancient Hindu text composed in the Sanskrit language. Macdonell's work on the text began in 1880, when he was appointed to the Boden Chair in Comparative Philology at the University of Oxford. This opportunity allowed him to specialize in the study of the ancient Indian Vedic language and literature.

Macdonell worked on the Rigveda diligently, comparing different texts of the text and carefully exploring their linguistic and literary features. His goal was to analyze the text through an academic and literary lens, in order to gain insight into how the text worked. Through his work, Macdonell was able to develop a comprehensive understanding of the composition and content of the Rigveda. He improved upon previous translations and recensions of the text, showing how cultural and religious ideas intertwined within the writing.

Macdonell was also able to provide significant information on the authors of the Rigveda and the social importance of their compositions. He demonstrated how their writing style indicated that the Rigveda was composed in a stylized, formulaic manner. He argued that this suggests the work was written in a very structured, organized way, rather than a free form improvisation. As such, his work has had a major impact on our understanding of the Rigveda and its composition.

Macdonell's greatest achievement in his work on the Rigveda was his legendary translation of the text. This translation, published in 1897, is a remarkable and influential piece of scholarship to this day. Macdonell believed that in order to understand the Rigveda adequately, it was essential to translate it into English. He was able to accomplish this with great success and his translation is the standard that is still used by many scholars today.

In conclusion, it is clear that Macdonell made significant contributions to our knowledge and understanding of the Rigveda, making his work on the text one of the most influential and important in the field of Vedic studies. His translation and recension of the Rigveda is a major source of information and his work has played a major role in how we think about the text today.

CHAPTER NINETEEN

AUTHOR GERALD LARSON AND RIGVEDA

Gerald Larson is a scholar in the field of Sanskrit and ancient Indian studies, well-known for his analyses of the Rigveda, the oldest and holiest of Vedic scriptures. Dr. Larson has made pioneering contributions to the field of Vedic studies, particularly in the areas of textual criticism, philology, and historical linguistics. His extensive research into the Rigveda has shed invaluable insight into this ancient text as well as providing important new interpretations.

Dr. Larson earned his Ph.D. in Sanskrit and South Asian Studies from Harvard University under the guidance of renowned Indologist Mary Grace Orr. He has served as the Robert and Gayle Spitzer distinguished professor of religious studies at Syracuse University since 1988 and has authored or edited several books and numerous articles on the Rigveda covering topics ranging from the history of literary interpretation to the analysis of linguistic structures.

Dr. Larson has compiled and analyzed thousands of manuscript sources to determine the development of the Rigveda over time. He argues that many of the previously held theories about the Rigveda's origin and relationship to other Vedic texts have been based on incomplete or neglected material and can now be re-examined with greater confidence. His rigorous examination of the hymns of the Rigveda from the earliest manuscripts has provided a better understanding of the compositional techniques employed by sacrificial priests in the ancient period.

Dr. Larson has also delved into the history and origins of the Rigveda, providing new evidence to dispute the Aryan Invasion Theory, which states that the Rigveda was composed by a people known as "Aryans" who migrated into the Indian subcontinent. He has argued that the internal evidence of the Rigveda itself reveals a more complex, heterogenous composition of early Indian culture and a less linear history of migration and invasion.

In addition to his work on the Rigveda, Dr. Larson is also a noted translator of classical Sanskrit literature and the author of several popular books on Hinduism and Vedanta. He continues to teach and lead research projects on a variety of topics related to the Rigveda and Indic religion in general. Dr. Larson's work on the Rigveda has helped broaden our knowledge and understanding of this ancient and sacred scripture, as well as providing a valuable source of information for scholars of South Asian studies throughout the world.

CHAPTER TWENTY

INDIAN SCHOLARS AND RIGVEDA

One of the oldest and most celebrated scriptures of ancient India, the Rigveda is known to have been compiled between 3000 and 2000 BCE. It is composed in an archaic language known as Vedic Sanskrit and its words and verses are believed to be immortal and timeless. The Rigveda contains numerous hymns and mantras, with each chapter devoted to a different god. It is said to contain the essence of all knowledge of the Vedas and fulfills important spiritual, philosophical and religious purposes.

Over the millennia, many Indian scholars and thinkers have written commentaries on the Rigveda and its importance for Hinduism and the wider religious and spiritual life of South Asia. This essay will discuss some of the most prominent of these scholars and the insights they provided.

One of the earliest known Indian scholars to investigate the Rigveda was Sayanacharya, who lived during the 6th and 7th centuries CE. He was a renowned linguist, philologist and Vedic commentator and he produced commentaries on the Rigveda and other Vedic textshe was heavily influenced by the Rigveda and its sacred language. His commentaries discussed the importance of Vedic Sanskrit, how to interpret and analyze the hymns and mantras, and how individual gods and concepts could be linked to larger cosmological and metaphysical ideas.

Another great Indian scholar who wrote commentaries on the Rigveda was Yaska, whose work is said to date from around the 5th century BCE. His writings, which are known as the Nirukta, are a set of philosophical and linguistic commentaries on the Rigveda. Yaska focused on how the language of the Rigveda could be used to convey complex ideas about the gods. He aimed to provide a comprehensive guide to Vedic notions of the divine and argued for the Rigveda's timelessness and unity of purpose.

The 19th century was a period of intense Vedic study and much work was done by Dayanand Saraswati, a renowned celibate scholar. He wrote a number of commentaries on the Rigveda and its language and philosophy. His writings were heavily influenced by the Upanishadic concepts of monism and ahimsa and his interpretation of the text focused on how the Vedas were part of a larger divinely inspired wisdom. He was also strongly critical of idol worship and popular religion, advocating for a more puritanical and rigorous ethical path.

The Rigveda has also inspired a large number of modern Indian scholars and commentators, such as Jaimini and Ved Vyas. Their work builds on the commentaries and interpretations of previous scholars but seeks to contextualize the Rigveda within a modern and scientific framework. Jaimini argued for a symbolic approach to the text, where certain passages could be read as parables, and Ved Vyas tried to understand the Rigveda's message.

CHAPTER TWENTY-ONE

SHANKARACHARYA'S COMMENTARIES ON RIGVEDA

Shankaracharya is considered one of the most important Hindu philosophers, who reinterpreted and revitalized the Vedic tradition in India during the 8th century. His commentaries on RigVeda played a crucial role in reviving and popularizing the Vedic religion.

Shankaracharya wrote commentaries on various Upanishads as well as on Brahma Sutras. He also wrote commentaries on various verses of RigVeda. His contribution to Vedic philosophy and interpretation is immense.

His main contribution to RigVeda is his commentaries on the hymns. He interpreted the verses in such a way that they could be understood both by the scholar as well as by the common people. He interpreted the verses in a dualistic fashion in order to show the ancient authorities from which he deduced his teachings and to show that the material world and its associated suffering were completely rooted in a spiritual reality.

Shankaracharya's interpretations focused mainly on the monism, non-dualism, and the ultimate reality of Brahman. He interpretated the verses in terms of the two fundamental categories i.e. the non-duality of Atma (Soul) and Brahma (God) and the duality of the material world which involves the material world and its associated suffering.

Shankaracharya's commentaries on RigVeda also provided insight into the ancient Vedic practices. He explained the rituals that were followed by the Vedic people and the philosophical implications of various hymns. He highlighted the importance of rituals in Vedic tradition and also clarified various rituals related to fire and sacrifice. He also explained various concepts related to the practices related to astrology, animal sacrifice, and Vedic kingship.

Shankaracharya's commentaries on RigVeda also sought to provide guidance to the common people on how to live their lives in accordance with the principles of Dharma. He explained the objectives of Dharma and the importance of righteous living. He further asserted that Dharma leads to liberation from the cycle of births and deaths and it was through the practice of Dharma that one could attain spiritual enlightenment.

Shankara's commentary on RigVeda is widely accepted as one of the most authentic interpretations of the Vedic philosophy. His commentaries highlighted the importance of spiritual practice, the need for righteous living, and the ultimate goal of seeking spiritual liberation from the cycle of births and deaths. His commentaries continue to influence the thinking of Hindu scholars and lay people alike and continue to remain relevant today.

CHAPTER TWENTY-TWO

SAYANACHARYA AND RIGVED

Sayanacharya is an important figure in Vedic literature, most famous for his impressive commentary of the Rig Veda. His works have played an important role in deciphering the language and composition of the Vedic tradition.

Sayanacharya is believed to have lived in the 8th century, though the exact dates of his life are uncertain. He belonged to a highly influential community of Advaita scholars and thinkers. He is considered to be a key figure in the development of Advaita Vedanta.

Sayanacharya's most famous work is his detail commentary on the Rig Veda. The commentary is composed of two different parts – the Bhashyakara and the Bhatodhara. In the Bhashyakara, Sayanacharya explains the meaning and significance of various hymns and verses from the Rig Veda. He expands on the symbolism and interpretation of rites, rituals and prayers of this ancient Hindu text.

In the Bhatodhara, Sayanacharya is more rigorous in his

study of the Rig Veda. He provides a clear, critical analysis of the sequence of Vedic rituals that are outlined in the text. He also proposes innovative theories on the implications of each and every ritual.

The best part about Sayanacharya's work is that he does not merely focus on a single aspect of the Rig Veda. Instead, he paints a broader picture of the multi-dimensional Vedic tradition and culture. He looks into the various aspects of Vedic life such as cosmic cycles, initiation rites and the connection between individuals and the Supreme Being.

Since its publication, Sayanacharya's commentary of the Rig Veda has become essential reading for scholars and students of the vedic tradition. Not only does it provide an invaluable insight into the rituals and hymns associated with the Rig Veda, but it also offers a fascinating glimpse into the world of 8th century India. His commentary serves as a reminder that Hinduism was and still is a unique, living tradition.

Although the exact dates of Sayanacharya's life are unknown, it is likely that he lived between the 8th and 9th centuries. His commentary of the Rig Veda is considered to be highly accurate and has served as an invaluable resource for scholars and researchers of this ancient Hindu text. All in all, Sayanacharya's work on the Rig Veda has preserved for modern readers an invaluable insight into the vedic tradition and culture of 8th century India.

CHAPTER TWENTY-THREE

ACHARYA YASKA AND RIGVED

Acharya Yaska, who lived around 8th century BCE, is widely credited for compiling the Vedic texts, known as the Nirukta. The Nirukta is a set of commentaries on the Vedic literature, made up of Vedic, Brahmanas and Sutra texts. It is widely believed that Acharya Yaska was the most learned in the Vedas, having mastered all its different branches.

The Nirukta is widely regarded as one of the most important texts of the Vedas. It helps in understanding the Vedas, and the commentaries explain the meanings of the words used in the Vedic literature, which often had an esoteric or hidden meaning. It is believed that the commentary helped to explain the deeper meaning of the Vedic texts, which would not have been possible without it.

The Nirukta also acts as a guide to other branches of Vedic studies such as the Puranas. It also serves as a source of information for the various rituals and sacrifices that are performed in the Vedic religion. One of the most important sections of the Nirukta is the Yaska Smriti, which deals with matters of penance and other religious practices.

The Nirukta is not a comprehensive text, but rather it is selective. The texts that were selected by Acharya Yaska for inclusion in the Nirukta were considered to be the most valuable sections of the Vedic literature. These texts needed to be studied with great care and to be interpreted with respect to the context in which they were written.

Acharya Yaska also wrote commentaries on the works of the great Vedic poets such as Maharishi Valmiki, Valmiki Ramayana and the Mahabharta. He also wrote commentaries on other sacred texts such as the Upanishads, the Vedanta Sutras, the Gita and the Veda Samhitas.

In addition to his work on the Vedic texts, Acharya Yaska was also involved in the fields of linguistics, grammar, phonetics and pragmatics. He wrote the celebrated Nirukta, which is one of the earliest works on the grammatical structure of the Sanskrit language. He is credited with formulating the notion of 'referents', which refers to the way in which words are used to refer to objects or concepts.

It is clear to see why Acharya Yaska's contributions to Vedic literature were so vast and influential. His work on the Vedic texts, commentaries and other sacred texts helped to shape the Vedic religion and its practices. He was an expert in his field and his works have greatly influenced the study of the Vedas and other religious texts.

CHAPTER TWENTY-FOUR

DAYANAND SARASWATI AND RIGVEDA

Dayanand Saraswati (1824 – 1883) was a philosopher, spiritual leader, and social reformer of India. He was one of the architects of the Indian Independence movement and is considered one of the earliest social reformers of modern India. He is also renowned for his views on the Vedas and was one of the key interpreters and proponents of the RigVeda in modern India.

Dayanand Saraswati had a firm belief in the infallibility of Vedas and considered them to be the divine command, given by the creator himself. He held that the RigVeda was the oldest text and the 'original and first book of knowledge of all times'. The term 'RigVeda' was originally just two words 'Rit' and 'Veda', which translates to 'knowledge of the righteous path'. The basic teaching of the Veda is that one must lead a morally principled life and work for the good of all. Dayanand Saraswati relied heavily on the Vedic scriptures, including the RigVeda, in his teachings and advocated a return to the Vedic way of life.

Dayanand Saraswati also spoke highly of the Rigveda in his writings. For example, he considered it to be the source of all knowledge and asserted that the knowledge derived from it was superior to that from any other text at the time. He argued that the RigVeda contained all the answers to the questions of life and that one should continually seek knowledge in order to progress spiritually and morally. Furthermore, he believed that by following the guidance of the RigVeda, one would lead a virtuous and meaningful life.

Dayanand Saraswati was of the opinion that the RigVeda was not just about rituals but about the eternal values of truth, kindness and justice. He argued that the essential verses of the Rigveda, if followed sincerely, could make the world full of peace and harmony. He also stressed the importance of maintaining a healthy balance between the forces of righteousness and evil. Additionally, Dayanand advocated preserving ancient traditions and customs as elucidated in the RigVeda. He called for the rising of the 'Arya Samaj', a movement based on the teachings of the Rigveda.

Dayanand was a great influence on the modern Indian thought process and his teachings had a lasting impact on the cultural identity of India. His views on the RigVeda have been widely accepted and his interpretation of the ancient text has become a cornerstone of modern India.

Through his works and teachings, Dayanand Saraswati succeeded in reviving interest in the RigVeda and ensuring its immortality for generations to come.

CHAPTER TWENTY-FIVE

VEDA VYAS AND RIGVEDA

The Rigveda is an aVEDA VYAS AND RIGVEDAncient Indian collection of Vedic Sanskrit hymns dedicated to the gods. It is one of the four Vedas, or religious texts, that is the oldest extant Indian text, dating back in its present form to around 1500–1200 BCE. The Rigveda is particularly important as it is composed of four parts, which are known as the Samhitas, or collections of hymns. The greatness of the Rigveda was recognized by the legendary sage Veda Vyasa, who is said to have composed it.

Veda Vyasa is the legendary author of the Rigveda, along with other monumental works such as the Mahabharata and the Upanishads. He is widely regarded by Hindus as an incarnation of the god Vishnu and the founder of numerous Hindu traditions and beliefs. Veda Vyasa created the Rigveda with the help of the four Rishis—or ancient sages—each of whom was associated with a specific type of knowledge. He arranged the Vedic hymns of the Rigveda into four compilations, called the Samhitas, or collections.

Veda Vyasa's authorship of the Rigveda is important for several reasons. First, it provides a framework for the further development of Hindu religious texts and ideas. Veda Vyasa's commentary on the Rigveda established a set of rituals and beliefs that were followed by subsequent generations and became the basis of Hinduism. It is also believed that Veda Vyasa compiled the Rigveda to preserve the spiritual knowledge that had been revealed to him. By organizing the Rigveda into four distinct Samhitas, Veda Vyasa enabled later readers to look at the individual hymns in isolation and appreciate their unique beauty.

The Rigveda, along with the other Vedas and the teachings of Veda Vyasa, form the core of Hinduism. Although the Rigveda is an ancient work, its spiritual content is still relevant today and provides guidance and inspiration to Hindu followers. Veda Vyasa is revered for his scholarly works, his inspiring and wise teachings, and his crucial role in the preservation of the Rigveda. He is credited with revealing the deepest truths of Vedic knowledge and for providing a comprehensive understanding of the spiritual path that has been followed by Hindus for thousands of years.

Contact

CONTACT

DR. JAGADEESH PILLAI

PhD in Vedic Science

Four Times Guinness World Record Holder

Winner of Mahatma Gandhi Vishwa Shanti Puraskar and
Global Peace Ambassador

9839093003

myrichindia@gmail.com

drjagadeeshpillai@facebook

drjagadeeshpillai@instagram

jagadeeshpillai@youtube

www. JAGADEESHPILLAI.com